Cultural Traditions in

Japan

Lynn
Peppas

Crabtree Publishing Company

www.crabtreebooks.com

Crabtree Publishing Company

www.crabtreebooks.com

Author: Lynn Peppas
Publishing plan research and development:
  Sean Charlebois, Reagan Miller
  Crabtree Publishing Company
Project coordinator: Kathy Middleton
Editors: Adrianna Morganelli, Crystal Sikkens
Proofreader: Kathy Middleton
Photo research: Allison Napier, Crystal Sikkens
Design: Margaret Amy Salter
Production coordinator: Margaret Amy Salter
Prepress technician: Margaret Amy Salter
Print coordinator: Katherine Berti

Cover: Japanese lanterns on a cherry blossom
tree (top); Kinkaku-ji, or Temple of the Golden
Pavilion, in Kyoto, Japan (center); Japanese New
Year decoration (bottom left); geisha (middle right);
Gion matsuri festival in Kyoto, Japan (middle left);
Japanese carp kites used for decoration on Children's
Day (top right); sushi (bottom right)

Title page: A Japanese women in a traditional
kimono by a cherry blossom tree

Photographs:
Alamy: © JTB Photo Communications, Inc: page 15 (bottom)
Kyodo/AP Images: page 25 (bottom)
© Toru Hanai/Reuters/Corbis: page 29
Dreamstime: page 28 (top right)
Fotolia: page 28 (top left)
iStockphoto: Kiyoshi Ota: page 30
Keystone Press: page 22 (left); © Natsuki Sakai/
  AFLO/Zumapress.com: page 31 (bottom)
Photodisc: page 7
Shutterstock: cover (top, top right, center, bottom left and
  right), pages 1, 6, 13, 14, 16, 17, 20, 28 (top and bottom);
  rudiuk: cover (geisha); Chiharu cover (middle left);
  J. Henning Buchholz: page 8; Chiharu: page 10;
  SeanPavonePhoto: page 18; Solodov Alexey:
  page 22 (right); Kobby Dagan: page 24; Attila JANDI:
  page 24–25 (background); Northfoto: page 31 (top)
Thinkstock: pages 4, 5, 9, 15 (top), 19, 26
Wikimedia Commons: page 13 (bottom); © Jnn: page 11;
  Sakura Chihaya: page 12; U.S. Navy photo by
  Photographer's Mate 2nd Class Jonathan R. Kulp:
  page 21; Douglas P Perkins: page 23; www8.cao.go.jp/
  intro/kunsho/english/bunka.html: page 25 (top);
  katorisi: page 27

Library and Archives Canada Cataloguing in Publication

Peppas, Lynn
    Cultural traditions in Japan / Lynn Peppas.

(Cultural traditions in my world)
Includes index.
Issued also in electronic format.
ISBN 978-0-7787-7586-7 (bound).--ISBN 978-0-7787-7593-5 (pbk.)

    1. Festivals--Japan--Juvenile literature. 2. Holidays--Japan--
Juvenile literature. 3. Japan--Social life and customs--Juvenile
literature. I. Title. II. Series: Cultural traditions in my world

GT4884.A2P47 2012   j394.26952   C2012-900668-8

Library of Congress Cataloging-in-Publication Data

Peppas, Lynn.
  Cultural traditions in Japan / Lynn Peppas.
    p. cm. -- (Cultural traditions in my world)
  Includes index.
  ISBN 978-0-7787-7586-7 (reinforced library binding : alk. paper) --
  ISBN 978-0-7787-7593-5 (pbk. : alk. paper) -- ISBN 978-1-4271-7865-7
  (electronic pdf) -- ISBN 978-1-4271-7980-7 (electronic html)
  1. Festivals--Japan--Juvenile literature. 2. Holidays--Japan--Juvenile literature.
  3. Japan--Social life and customs--Juvenile literature. I. Title.

GT4884.A2P47 2012
394.26952--dc23

2012003078

Crabtree Publishing Company

www.crabtreebooks.com   1-800-387-7650

Printed in the U.S.A./03013/SN20130122

Published in Canada
Crabtree Publishing
616 Welland Ave.
St. Catharines, ON
L2M 5V6

Published in the United States
Crabtree Publishing
PMB 59051
350 Fifth Avenue, 59th Floor
New York, New York 10118

Published in the United Kingdom
Crabtree Publishing
Maritime House
Basin Road North, Hove
BN41 1WR

Published in Australia
Crabtree Publishing
3 Charles Street
Coburg North
VIC 3058

Contents

Welcome to Japan

Japan is a country that is made up of many **islands** that are close to one another in the Pacific Ocean. There are also many mountains in Japan. Japanese people live on the flat lands between the mountains. Japan has a **population** of 127 million people. That is a lot of people living in an area that is almost the size of the state of Montana.

Many Japanese people follow the fashions from the United States. They call this Western-style.

Most Japanese people live in large, modern cities. They celebrate their culture with festivals and holidays on different days throughout the year. During holidays and festivals many follow **ancient** traditions that have been passed down for thousands of years. Traditions are customs and beliefs that are handed down from **ancestors**.

Did You Know? Bowing can be used to show **respect**, say thank you, apologize, or show affection.

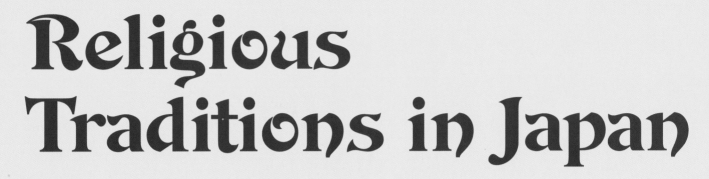

Religious Traditions in Japan

The two main religions in Japan are Shinto and Buddhism. People celebrate some festivals and holidays in different ways according to their religion. Shinto religion teaches that all things in nature such as the Sun, mountains, rivers, and all living things have a **spirit**. Japanese pray to these spirits to protect them from harm. On religious holidays, they visit a Shinto shrine to celebrate.

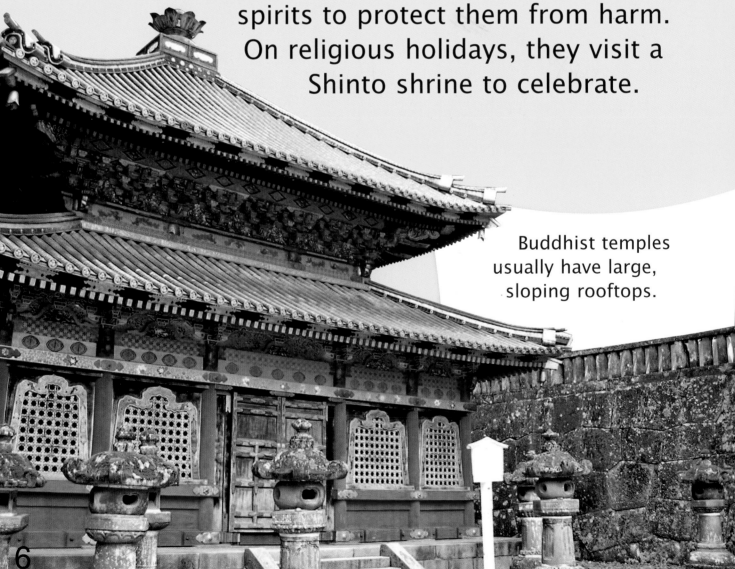

Buddhist temples usually have large, sloping rooftops.

Shinto shrines are often built on mountains or near waterways and are believed to have the natural spirit living inside them.

Japanese people who follow Buddhism believe in one God whose teachings came by a messenger named Buddha. In Japan, sculptures of Buddha are carved into rock on mountains. Festivals such as the Flower Festival (see pages 16-17) are Buddhist festivals.

Family Occasions

Over 50 years ago, most marriages in Japan were arranged. Arranged means that the parents choose who their children will marry. Today Japanese people choose their own husband or wife. Brides often wear white makeup and white dresses. They often wear traditional white headpieces that circle the top of the head like a band.

A Japanese bride wears white to show purity. A groom is often dressed in a traditional black **kimono**.

Long ago, it was a tradition that all people in Japan celebrated their birthdays on January 1. Everyone turned a year older on New Year's Day. A person's true birth date was not important. Today, people in Japan celebrate on their actual birth dates. Traditions have changed and birthdays are now celebrated much the same as they are in North America.

Did You Know?
People in Japan use chopsticks to eat their food. Chopsticks are long, thin, wooden sticks.

Japanese people have taken on North American birthday traditions such as sharing birthday cake for the special day.

Japanese New Year

New Year's Day is the most important holiday in Japan. It is a **national** holiday. People get January 1 off of work and children get the day off of school. Many businesses and schools close for a three-day holiday. Children often receive gifts of money on this day.

At the Shurijo Castle in Okinawa, Japan, performers reenact a traditional New Year's Day ceremony where the king, queen, and royal family attended.

People in Japan pay their bills and finish their work before New Year's Day to start their new year with no worries. Homes in Japan are cleaned before New Year's Day. People cook their New Year's Day dinners before New Year's Day so that no cooking has to be done. People in Japan believe that what a person does on New Year's Day will affect their year ahead.

Did You Know?
A popular Japanese tradition for the New Year is to send New Year's Day greetings on postcards called *nengajō* to friends and family members.

Spring Festival

The Spring Festival is called *Setsubun* in Japanese. It is an ancient festival that celebrates the coming of springtime. It is held every year on the day before spring, which is February 3 or 4. It is not a national holiday. People in Japan do not get the day off work or school.

In the evening of Setsubun, people eat uncut Eho-Maki, or lucky direction rolls. The rolls are eaten while facing the lucky compass direction, determined by the year's **zodiac** symbol.

During the festival, people will throw beans at anyone wearing a demon mask and shout, "Demons out, happiness in."

Did You Know?
After throwing beans, people in Japan pick up the same number of beans as their age and eat them!

Setsubun is known as the bean-throwing festival. The tradition began thousands of years ago. People threw beans to scare off evil spirits. Today bean-throwing ceremonies are held at religious temples or shrines.

Sometimes celebrities will be invited to participate at bigger shrines where they throw beans along with candies, or small envelopes of money.

Doll Festival

Young girls in Japan have their own special festival. March 3 marks the Doll Festival, or Hina Matsuri, in Japan. Matsuri means festival in Japanese. The Doll Festival is thousands of years old and celebrates the health and happiness of girls.

Some doll collections have special dolls that have been handed down from their ancestors.

Today in Japan, girls **display**, or show, their family's doll collection during the Doll Festival. Girls dress and decorate these special dolls. Often Japanese girls wear their kimonos and get together with each other to play games. They celebrate with traditional foods such as rice cakes and rice crackers.

Girls dress up in their traditional kimonos during Doll Festival.

Flower Festival

Japan's Flower Festival is a religious festival. It is held on April 8, the birthday of a man named Buddha who was a prophet, or messenger, from God. Buddha lived thousands of years ago. He started the religion called Buddhism.

Did You Know?
The Flower Festival takes place during spring when the cherry blossoms come out on cherry trees. This is why it is called the Flower Festival.

During the Flower Festival people in Japan decorate statues of Buddha and take them to Buddhist temples where they **worship**. A tradition is to pour sweet tea over Buddha's head as though you are bathing a newborn baby.

Flower arranging is a form of art in Japan. Called ikebana, it must be done in silence to encourage the appreciation of the beauty of nature.

17

Golden Week

Golden Week is a group of different holidays in Japan that begin on April 29 and end on May 5. They are national holidays when most people get the time off of work, and children do not have to go to school.

Many people travel during Golden Week because they have so many days off in a row.

The first holiday in Golden Week is called Showa Day. It is celebrated because it is the birthday of **Emperor** Showa. May 3 is Constitution Day in Japan. A constitution is a set of rules that rule a country. May 4 is Greenery Day. Just like it sounds, it is a day to celebrate nature and the **environment**. May 5 is Children's Day. Long ago it was a festival day for boys, but today it celebrates all young people in Japan.

Did You Know?
Samurai warrior dolls and carp kites are decorations used in Japan on Children's Day. Both represent power and strength.

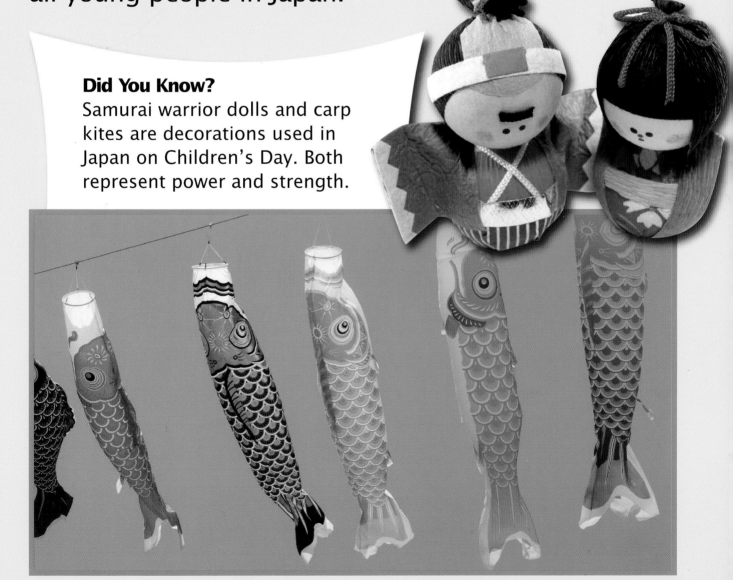

19

Obon Festival

The Obon Festival is sometimes celebrated from July 13 to 15 and sometimes from August 13 to 16. It is the second-biggest holiday in Japan and an important time to spend with family. Many use these days to travel to their hometowns or spend time with family. People believe that the spirits of family members that have died return to their homes during this time. Some people visit the graves of their deceased relatives to clean the sites and call the relatives home.

To help the spirits find their way, lanterns are placed near gates, doorways, or inside homes.

On the last evening of the Obon Festival, people gather to send the spirits of their relatives back to rest. Lanterns are lit and set in a river to float down to the ocean. It is believed the spirits travel with the lanterns. Communities also hold outdoor dances and parties on this night. Dances usually take place at parks, gardens, temples, or shrines, and people come dressed in their summer kimonos.

Did You Know
The Obon Festival is sometimes called the Mid-Summer Festival because it is celebrated in the middle of the summer. Some people give mid-summer presents to special people in their lives.

The Obon Festival is also sometimes referred to as the Festival of Lanterns. Lanterns are used to guide spirits home and back, as shown here in Sasebo, Nagasaki Prefecture, Japan.

Health and Sports Day

Japanese people know it is important to keep fit and healthy. They even go so far as to celebrate a holiday called Health and Sports Day. It falls on different dates every year, but is always held on the second Monday in October. Health and Sports Day is a national holiday. That means most people get the day off work and children get the day off of school.

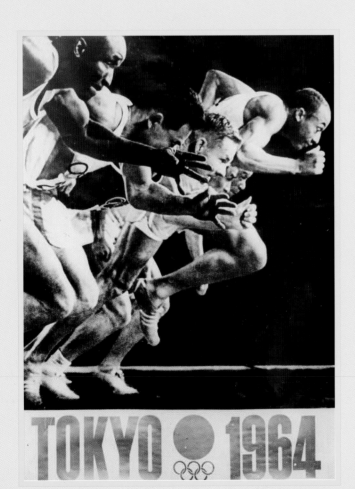

Did You Know?
Health and Sports Day is held to remember the Summer Olympics that were held in Toyko in October 1964.

Sports Day, as it is sometimes called, is a recent holiday that began in 1966. In Japanese cities people organize parades of teams. These teams compete in Olympic-style sports events. Children participate in physical activities such as ball games, gymnastics, and tug-of-war.

Some schools in Japan hold their field days on this day each year.

Culture Day

People in Japan celebrate their culture with a holiday called Culture Day. It is a national holiday held every year on November 3. Most people get the day off work and children get the day off of school. The first Culture Day took place in 1946. It is a modern holiday that helps Japanese people remember their older traditions, too.

People are participating in an archery contest on Culture Day in Toyko, Japan.

Culture Day encourages people to celebrate Japan's culture. Many go to art or dance shows. Larger cities hold festivals and parades. Many dress in traditional kimonos. It is also a day when awards are given to artists and students in Japan.

The Order of Culture is a Japanese award given by the emperor of Japan to a person who has contributed to the arts, sciences, or culture of Japan.

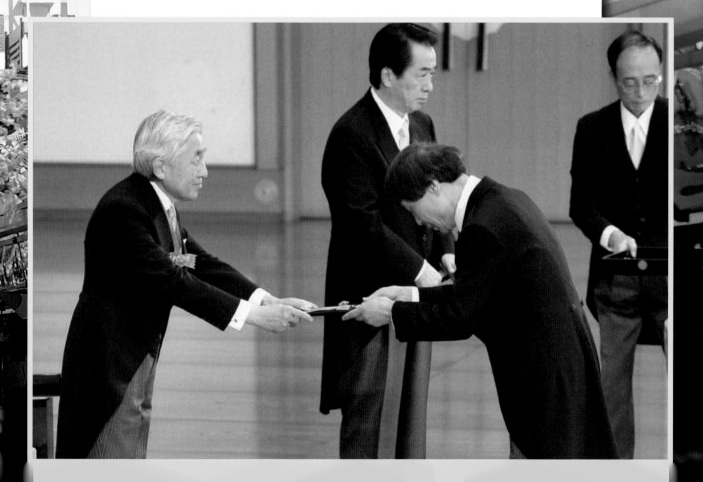

7-5-3 Festival

Japanese children celebrate turning seven, five, and three years old in Japan. It is called the 7-5-3 Festival, and it takes place on November 15. Some years it is celebrated on the weekend closest to November 15. People do not get time off of work or school.

Japanese children dress in their best clothing or traditional kimonos on this day.

Did You Know?
Odd numbers such as seven, five, and three are thought to be lucky in Japan.

Sticks of red and white thousand-year candy are given to children celebrating the 7-5-3 Festival.

Did You Know?
The 7-5-3 Festival is called Shichi-go-san in Japan. *Shichi* means seven, *go* means five, and *san* means three in Japanese.

The 7-5-3 Festival is a religious holiday when Japanese children and their parents go to a Shinto shrine to get special blessings. People pray for good health and a long life for their children. They also get long sticks of red and white candy called thousand-year candy. The candy is given to wish children a long life.

Labor Thanksgiving Day

Thanksgiving Day in Japan is a **harvest** festival held every year on November 23. It is sometimes called Labor Thanksgiving Day. On this national holiday in Japan many get the day off work and school.

Did You Know?
Many young students give gifts they have made to local police officers to say thank you for the work they do to keep their cities safe.

Labor Thanksgiving Day is an ancient holiday. Long ago, people gave thanks for crops such as rice. For thousands of years the emperor of Japan held a religious service to give thanks for the rice harvest. Today, people also celebrate the work they do throughout the year. Families enjoy the day off together. Some visit festivals held in cities such as Nagano.

A young girl admires the display of vegetables created to celebrate the year's harvest at a shrine in Tokyo on Labor Thanksgiving Day.

Emperor's Birthday

Japanese people celebrate the birthday of the emperor in power. An emperor is a person who rules over a country such as Japan. The emperor's birthday has been celebrated in Japan for thousands of years. Today it is celebrated as a national holiday. Many people get the day off of work or school.

The present emperor of Japan is Emperor Akihito. He has been emperor since 1989.

Today the emperor's birthday is celebrated on December 23—the birthday of Emperor Akihito. On this day the gates to the Imperial Palace where the emperor lives are opened. Crowds of people come to wish the emperor happy birthday and wave Japanese flags. The emperor waves to the people from his palace balcony.

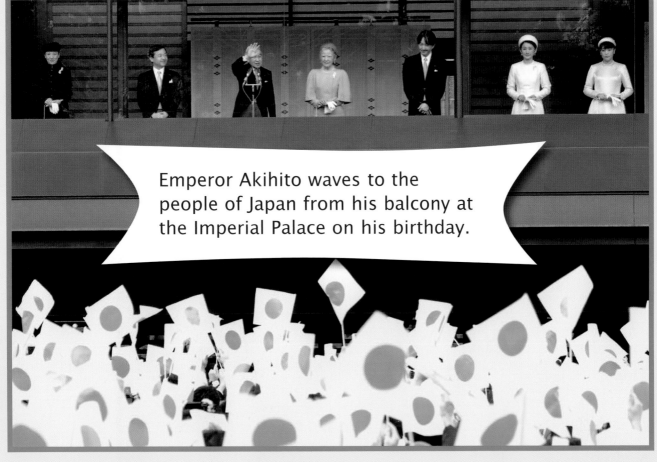

Emperor Akihito waves to the people of Japan from his balcony at the Imperial Palace on his birthday.

Glossary

ancestor A relative who was alive in the past

ancient Having been around for thousands of years

display To put out so that others can see

emperor The ruler of an empire, country, or nation

environment A person's surroundings

harvest The season when crops are gathered

islands A body of land surrounded by water

kimono A traditional robe or gown with wide sleeves kept together with a thick belt in the middle

national Things that have to do with a country or nation

population The number of people living in an area

respect Paying special attention to a person

spirit The soul of a dead person

worship To practice the traditions of a religion such as praying

zodiac An imaginary belt in the heavens that is divided into 12 parts

Index